## SOME THINGS ARE WORTH FIGHTING FOR

CREATED BY TIERCE GREEN

# FIGHT CLUB

Published by Good Feed Media


ISBN: 979-8-9921538-1-1

This book supports the video content created and presented by Tierce Green. There are twelve sessions in the series. The average length of each session is about 30 minutes.

Video sessions for this series are completely FREE within the **Good Feed Media** App. There is no obligation to pay for anything, but you have the opportunity to help us KEEP IT FREE by paying it forward.

Order additional copies of this resource and high-definition videos of this series for public viewing from Good Feed Media.

ORDER RESOURCES AND DOWNLOAD THE APP AT GOODFEEDMEDIA.COM

Good Feed Media is a division of Tierce Green Ministries, Inc.

Video production by Layne Laughter.

Distributed by:

Tierce Green Ministries, Inc.
The Woodlands, TX 77393
tiercegreen.com

## [PART ONE]



## [PART TWO]

# ABOUT THE CONTENT

The Apostle Paul encouraged a young man named Timothy to pursue righteousness, godliness, faith, love, endurance, and gentleness. He challenged him to fight the good fight of the faith. **Fight Club: Some Things Are Worth Fighting For** clarifies what it looks like for men to build a strong and active faith today. It was created for a seasonal gathering of men called The Quest.

The content was filmed at Chad Robichaux's Gracie Baja Jiu-Jitsu studio in The Woodlands, Texas. Chad went on to become the President & Founder of Mighty Oaks Warrior Programs and the Director of Veteran Affairs for Serving California, two non-profit organizations dedicated to helping our combat heroes suffering from the unseen wounds of combat stress and PTSD. The MOWP Edition of Fight Club was highly effective in helping many combat heroes find their way home.

All of the video sessions can be conveniently viewed on the Good Feed Media App, but a fundamental rule in Fight Club is that no man fights alone. While there can be some value in watching the sessions by yourself and making notes in this workbook, it would be wise to go through this series with other men and process the principles together. You need their perspective, encouragement, and support. They need the same from you.

# ABOUT THE AUTHOR

Tierce Green has over 45 years of professional ministry experience, including 30 years as a full-time speaker for conferences and retreats and 15 years of local church ministry. He served as a Student Pastor in a church of 1,200 and an Executive Pastor in a church of 12,000, where he led over a thousand men each week for seven years in a seasonal gathering called The Quest in The Woodlands, Texas.

Tierce is on the presentation team of **33 The Series** for Authentic Manhood, which has reached over three million men worldwide. He is the Director of **Authentic Manhood Initiative,** coaching leaders to reach men with the principles of biblical manhood. He is also the Director of **Good Feed Media**, creating quality disciple-making content freely available on the Good Feed Media App.

Tierce and his wife, Dana, have one daughter, Anna, and live in The Woodlands, TX.

# 5 RULES & 5 PROMISES

## I. INTRODUCTION

A. History of Gracie Brazilian Jiu Jitsu:

- Helio Gracie
  - First sports hero in Brazilian history
  - Dedicated family man who exemplified a healthy lifestyle
  - Epitome of courage, discipline, and determination
  - An inspiration to people everywhere

**THE JIU-JITSU THAT I CREATED WAS DESIGNED TO GIVE THE WEAK ONES A CHANCE TO FACE THE HEAVY AND STRONG.** – Grand Master Helio Gracie

B. **Our Goal:** Learn techniques and principles to face some heavy and strong opponents:

- Anger, rage, selfishness, materialism, fear, greed, lust, pornography, passivity, boyishness, laziness, self-righteousness, and a very real sinister force that is at work behind it all.

## II. WELCOME TO FIGHT CLUB

A. "How much can you know about yourself if you've never been in a fight?" – Tyler Durdan / *Fight Club*, the movie

B. It's through our struggles that we are developed into the men we are designed to be.

- James 1:2-4 // Consider it a sheer gift, friends, when tests and challenges come at you from all sides. You know that under pressure, your faith-life is forced into the open and shows its true colors. So don't try to get out of anything prematurely. Let it do its work so you become mature and well-developed, not deficient in any way. (The Message)

## III. THE FIVE RULES OF FIGHT CLUB

1. YOU DO NOT TALK ABOUT FIGHT CLUB

    - You must first pass the test of authenticity and respect the rule of confidentiality.
    - Luke 6:46 // Why do you call me, "Lord, Lord," and do not do what I say? (NIV)

2. NO MAN FIGHTS ALONE

    - We need other men to achieve our common goal of authentic manhood.
    - *Locking Arms: God's Design for Masculine Friendships* by Stu Weber
    - Ecclesiastes 4:9-10 // Two are better than one, because they have a good return for their labor: If either of them falls down, one can help the other up. But pity anyone who falls and has no one to help them up. (NIV)

3. EVERY MAN MUST FIGHT

    - Real men reject passivity.
    - Real men know and name their opponents.
    - 1 Corinthians 9:26-27 // I do not run like someone running aimlessly; I do not fight like a boxer beating the air. No, I strike a blow to my body and make it my slave so that after I have preached to others, I myself will not be disqualified for the prize. (NIV)

4. ONLY TRUE CONTENDERS ALLOWED

    - Real manhood requires a willingness to be real.

- Matthew 23:27-28 // Woe to you, teachers of the law and Pharisees, you hypocrites! You are like whitewashed tombs, which look beautiful on the outside but on the inside are full of the bones of the dead and everything unclean. In the same way, on the outside you appear to people as righteous but on the inside you are full of hypocrisy and wickedness. (NIV)

5. MAXIMUM REPS ARE REQUIRED

    - Every man who signs up must show up.

## IV. FIVE PROMISES FOR EVERY MAN WHO GOES THE DISTANCE

1. You will gain a broader perspective and a better understanding of the spiritual battle in which we are all engaged.

2. You will discover that you are not alone in the fight.

3. You will have the opportunity to build strong friendships with other men who are pursuing the same goal.

4. You will identify key moves to strengthen your core and support your quest for authentic manhood.

5. You will develop your own personalized fight plan for facing your biggest challenges to authentic manhood.

    - FIGHT PLAN: PAGE 95

## GUIDELINES FOR DISCUSSION

[1] DON'T RETEACH THE LESSON

[2] DON'T DOMINATE THE DISCUSSION

[3] BE SURE EVERYONE HAS A CHANCE TO TALK IF THEY WANT TO

## TALK ABOUT IT

1. Take a few minutes for everyone to be introduced.
2. What interested you the most about Fight Club? What expectations do you have?
3. Which of the 5 Rules and 5 Promises excite or concern you the most?
4. Have you ever had contact with a poser or a pretender? What was your experience?
5. Who has been there for you when you have fallen or been knocked out?

# NOTES

# WHY MEN NEED TO FIGHT

## I. ROUND 1 RECAP

A. 5 RULES OF FIGHT CLUB

1. YOU DO NOT TALK ABOUT FIGHT CLUB. You must first pass the test of authenticity and respect the rule of confidentiality.

2. NO MAN FIGHTS ALONE. We need other men to achieve our common goal of authentic manhood.

3. EVERY MAN MUST FIGHT. Real men reject passivity, and real men know and name their opponents.

4. ONLY TRUE CONTENDERS ALLOWED. Real manhood requires a willingness to be real.

5. MAXIMUM REPS ARE REQUIRED. Everyone who signs up must show up.

B. 5 PROMISES IF YOU GO THE DISTANCE

1. You will gain a broader perspective and a better understanding of the spiritual battle in which we are all engaged.

2. You will discover that you are not alone in the fight.

3. You will have the opportunity to build strong friendships with other men who are pursuing the same goal.

4. You will identify key moves to strengthen your core and support your quest for authentic manhood.

5. You will develop your own personalized fight plan for facing your biggest challenges to authentic manhood.

   - FIGHT PLAN: PAGE 95

## II. WHY MEN NEED TO FIGHT

A. MANHOOD TODAY HAS BECOME AN ABSTRACT CONCEPT.

- 1 Corinthians 13:11 // When I was a child, I talked like a child, I thought like a child, I reasoned like a child. When I became a man, I put childish ways behind me. (NIV)

1. Our perspective is distorted.

   - One extreme: Men are superior.
   - Another extreme: Men are a joke.

2. The biblical role of men has been diluted.

   - Mistake #1: When the Bible says that men and women are equal, it means they are the same.
   - Mistake #2: To love his wife the way Christ loved the church and gave himself up for it, a man will have to give up his role as the leader, or head.

3. The concept of manhood is so abstract that men are confused.

   - Proverbs 29:18 // Where there is no vision, the people are unrestrained ... (NASB)
   - 1 Timothy 4:12 // Don't let anyone look down on you because you are young, but set an example for the believers in speech, in life, in love, in faith and in purity. (NIV)

B. MEN ARE STUCK IN PROLONGED ADOLESCENCE.

C. THE HEALTH OF OUR SOCIETY DEPENDS ON IT.

*The central problem of every society is to define appropriate roles for its men.*
– Margaret Mead, Cultural Anthropologist

**THE CONCEPT OF MANHOOD**

**DISTORTED AND DILUTED = INCONSEQUENTIAL AND UNNECESSARY**

*Women may not find this surprising, but one of the most persistent and frustrating problems in evolutionary biology is the male. Specifically, where did he come from, and why doesn't he just go away?*

Natalie Angier, New York Times Columnist

## TALK ABOUT IT

1. What is your response to the statement in the box at the end of this outline by New York Times Columnist, Natalie Angier?
2. At what point in your life do you remember thinking: "Now I am a man!" Why did you think that?
3. Describe examples of manhood (good or bad) that you remember when you were a child or when you were a teenager.
4. What is one thing that challenged you the most from this session?

# NOTES

# NOTES

# OUR COMMON ENEMY

## I. ROUND 2 RECAP

A. Why men need to fight.

1. Manhood today has become an abstract concept:

- Our perspective is distorted.
- The biblical role of men has been diluted.
- Men are confused.

2. Men are stuck in a prolonged adolescence.

3. The health of our society depends on it.

B. Men are supposed to be producers, not just consumers.

C. Real men are defined by the legacy, the life and the fruit that comes out of them, not by what they take in.

## II. WHAT IS REALLY GOING ON?

A. Since the beginning of time, a dark spiritual force has been at work against us.

- Ephesians 6:12 // For our struggle is not against flesh and blood, but against the rulers, against the authorities, against the powers of this dark world, and against the spiritual forces of evil in the heavenly realms. (NIV)

B. The Bible clearly identifies our common enemy as Satan, or the Devil.

- 1 Peter 5:8-9 // Be self-controlled and alert. Your enemy the devil prowls around like a roaring lion looking for someone to devour. Resist him, standing firm in the faith, because you know that your brothers throughout the world are undergoing the same kind of sufferings. (NIV)

- Luke 22:31-32// Satan has asked to sift each of you like wheat. But I have pleaded in prayer for you, Simon, that your faith should not fail. So when you have repented and turned to me again, strengthen your brothers. (NLT)

## III. KNOW THE ENEMY

1 John 2:14-17 // I write to you, fathers, because you have known him who is from the beginning. I write to you, young men, because you are strong, and the word of God lives in you, and you have overcome the evil one.

Do not love the world or anything in the world. If anyone loves the world, the love of the Father is not in him. For everything in the world—the cravings of sinful man, the lust of his eyes and the boasting of what he has and does—comes not from the Father but from the world.

The world and its desires pass away, but the man who does the will of God lives forever. (NIV)

## ANALYZE THE STRATEGY

A. PART ONE: The Lust of the Flesh.

1. It is primarily a blow to the  body.

    - 1 Corinthians 6:19-20 // Do you not know that your body is a temple of the Holy Spirit who is in you, whom you have received from God? You are not your own; you were bought at a price. Therefore honor God with your body. (NIV)

2. The objective is to pervert our physical desires.

3. To pervert something is to use it in a way that distorts its created purpose.

B. PART TWO: The Lust of the Eyes.

1. It is primarily a blow to the mind.

2. A skewed perspective: We measure our life by temporary things.

3. We are defined by our possessions.

C. PART THREE: The Pride of Life.

James 4:6 // ... God opposes the proud but gives grace to the humble. (NIV)

1. Keeps us from admitting to ourselves that we need help.

2. Keeps us from asking others for help.

3. The ultimate blow is an eternal blow to our soul.

## IV. 8 MOVES TO GAIN POSITION OVER OUR COMMON ENEMY

A. Submit and resist.

- James 4:7 // Submit yourselves, then, to God. Resist the devil and he will flee from you. (NIV)

B. Rest and relaxation.

- Genesis 2:2 // By the seventh day God had finished the work he had been doing, so on the seventh day he rested from all his work. (NIV)

C. Simplify your life.

- Hebrews 12:1 // ...let us throw off everything that hinders and the sin that so easily entangles, and let us run with perseverance the race marked out for us. (NIV)

D. Pursue financial freedom.

- Deuteronomy 28:12 // The Lord will open the heavens, the storehouse of his bounty, to send rain on your land in season and to bless all the work of your hands. You will lend to many nations but will borrow from none. (NIV)

E. Stay connected.

- Ecclesiastes 4:9-12 // Two are better than one ... If one falls down, his friend can help him up ... Though one may be overpowered, two can defend themselves. A cord of three strands is not quickly broken. (NIV)

F. Meditate on scripture.

- Psalm 119:11 // I have hidden your word in my heart that I might not sin against you. (NIV)

G. Turn and run.

- 1 Corinthians 10:13 // ... when you are tempted, he will also provide a way out so that you can stand up under it. (NIV)

H. The presence of Jesus Christ.

Matthew 28:20 // ... I am with you always, to the very end of the age. (NIV)

## EVERY MAN'S PROMISE

And everyone who calls on the name of the Lord will be saved.

Acts 2:21

## TALK ABOUT IT

1. What is the most significant thing you learned in this session?
2. How have you seen the lust of the flesh, the lust of the eyes, and the pride of life at work in your life? Which one(s) have you struggled with the most?
3. Of the eight moves given to gain position over our common enemy, which one(s) do you think will be the most difficult for you to master? Why?
4. Personal Application: What can you add to your strategy to help you fight against our common enemy today? What needs to be integrated into your Personal Fight Plan?

# NOTES

# NOTES

# CHARACTER

## I. INTRODUCTION

A. If you want to be a man of character, you will have to fight for it.

- 1 Peter 5:8 // Be alert and of sober mind. Your enemy the devil prowls around like a roaring lion looking for someone to devour.

B. A heads-up and a promise:

- John 10:10 // The thief comes only to steal and kill and destroy; I have come that they may have life, and have it to the full. (NIV)

## II. WHAT IS CHARACTER?

> **CHARACTER IS THE WILL TO DO WHAT IS RIGHT, AS DEFINED BY GOD, REGARDLESS OF PERSONAL COST.**
>
> Andy Stanley, Louder Than Words

A. Character is a pre-decision to do what is right.

B. What is right is determined by God.

C. A man of character does what is right because it is right, not because it is convenient.

D. An Old Testament example of character:

- Joshua 24:14-15 // Now fear the Lord and serve him with all faithfulness. Throw away the gods your ancestors worshiped beyond the Euphrates River and in Egypt, and serve the Lord. But if serving the Lord seems undesirable to you, then choose for yourselves this day whom you will serve, whether the gods your ancestors served beyond the Euphrates, or the gods of the Amorites, in whose land you are living. But as for me and my household, we will serve the Lord.

## III. THE PROFILE

**LORD, WHO MAY DWELL IN YOUR SANCTUARY?**
**WHO MAY LIVE ON YOUR HOLY HILL?**
Psalm 15:1

A. A Man of **INTEGRITY**.

- Psalm 15:2a // He whose walk is blameless ... (NIV)

B. A Man of **ACTION**.

- Psalm 15:2b/ /... and who does what is righteous ... (NIV)

C. A Man of **HONESTY**.

- Psalm 15:2c // ... who speaks the truth from his heart ... (NIV)

D. A Man of **ENCOURAGEMENT**.

- Psalm 15:3/ /... and has no slander on his tongue, who does his neighbor no wrong and casts no slur on his fellowman ... (NIV)

E. A Man of **HONOR**.

- Psalm 15:4a // ... who despises a vile man but honors those who fear the Lord. (NIV)

F. A Man of **HIS WORD**.

- Psalm 15:4b // ... who keeps his oath even when it hurts ... (NIV)

G. A Man of **GENEROSITY**.

- Psalm 15:5a // ... who lends his money without usury and does not accept a bribe against the innocent ... (NIV)

## IV. THE PROMISE

**HE WHO DOES THESE THINGS WILL NEVER BE SHAKEN.**

Psalm 15:5b

A. The ability to bounce back.

B. Failure is not fatal.

- Psalm 37:23-24 // If the Lord delights in a man's way, he makes his steps firm. Though he stumble, he will not fall, for the Lord upholds him with his hand. (NIV)

## V. CHARACTER KILLERS

A. Standards that are flexible.

- Proverbs 11:3 // The integrity of the upright guides them, but the unfaithful are destroyed by their duplicity (NIV)

B. A blurred vision of manhood.

- Proverbs 29:18 // Where there is no vision, the people are unrestrained ... (NIV)

C. Shortcuts to manhood and maturity.

- James 1:4 // So don't try to get out of anything prematurely. Let it do its work so you become mature and well developed, not deficient in any way. (The Message)

- Romans 5:3-4 // ... we know that suffering produces perseverance; perseverance, character; and character, hope. (NIV)

D. An unguarded mind.

- Romans 12:2 // Do not conform any longer to the pattern of this world, but be transformed by the renewing of your mind... (NIV)

- 2 Corinthians 10:5 // ... take captive every thought to make it obedient to Christ. (NIV)

E. Friends who are foolish.

- Proverbs 13:20 // He who walks with the wise grows wise, but a companion of fools suffers harm. (NIV)

- 1 Corinthians 15:33 // Do not be misled. Bad company corrupts good character. (NIV)

F. A disconnection from authentic relationships with other men.

- Proverbs 14:12 // There is a way that seems right to a man, but in the end it leads to death. (NIV)

- Proverbs 15:22 // Plans fail for lack of counsel, but with many advisers they succeed. (NIV)

## TALK ABOUT IT

1. Who do you know that has modeled the traits from our CHARACTER PROFILE? Describe what you have seen and experienced in them.

2. Which of the seven character traits appeal to you the most? Which ones intimidate you?

3. Who have you known that was knocked out, but they got back up and achieved an even greater influence?

4. Which of the six character killers do you need help with the most?

# NOTES

# NOTES

# MARGIN

## I. WHAT IS MARGIN?

**MARGIN IS THE AMOUNT AVAILABLE BEYOND WHAT IS NECESSARY.**

– Andy Stanley

A. Divided and Disturbed: The Story of Mary & Martha (Luke 10:38-42)

B. Before you can determine what is **available**, you must first determine what is **necessary**.

C. We are driven by what we determine to be necessary.

## II. SEVEN MARKS OF A HURRIED FAMILY

(Adapted from *Little House on the Freeway* by Tim Kimmel)

A. We're so busy we can't relax.

B. We're uncomfortable with quiet.

C. We're seldom satisfied with what we have.

D. We live with shifting situational standards.

E. We are over-worked and under-appreciated.

F. We worry about things we can't control.

G. We aren't happy unless we are successful.

## III. MAKING THE MOST OF OUR TIME

Ephesians 5:15-17 // Be very careful, then, how you live – not as unwise but as wise, making the most of every opportunity, because the days are evil. Therefore do not be foolish, but understand what the Lord's will is. (NIV)

A. If you can't find margin, you will need to fight for it.

B. Fighting for margin could mean:

1. Saying no to many good things so you can say yes to the best things.

2. Turning down a promotion if it is going to negatively impact you or your family.

3. Negotiating for more vacation time instead of an increase in salary.

4. Limiting the use of technology.

5. Learning to be a better leader.

    - Exodus 18:17-19 // Moses' father-in-law replied, "What you are doing is not good. You and these people who come to you will only wear yourselves out. The work is too heavy for you; you cannot handle it alone. Listen now to me and I will give you some advice, and may God be with you ... "

6. Scheduling margin on your calendar.

C. Ask God for wisdom to make right choices.

- James 1:5 // If any of you lacks wisdom, he should ask God ... and it will be given to him. (NIV)

D. Before adding something to your schedule, learn to ask the best question: IS IT WISE?

- Ephesians 5:15-17 // Be very careful, then, how you live – not as unwise but as wise ... (NIV)

## THE BEST QUESTION

IS IT WISE IN LIGHT OF ...

*... what I value most?*

*... our current family situation?*

*... the struggles in my marriage?*

*... our financial deficit?*

*... our emotional deficit?*

## TALK ABOUT IT

1. What is the most significant thing you learned in this session?
2. Which of the SEVEN MARKS OF A HURRIED FAMILY can you identify with the most?
3. With regards to fighting for margin, which of the six items on the list would be the most beneficial to you? Which are the most challenging?
4. How can learning to ask THE BEST QUESTION help you create margin? What challenges do you see?

# NOTES

# NOTES

# MONEY & POSSESSIONS

## I. WHAT THE BIBLE SAYS ABOUT MONEY & POSSESSIONS

A. Jesus never condemned people for being rich.

B. The Scriptures do not condemn the possession or accumulation of money.

C. The Bible has GOOD THINGS to say about money and possessions.

1. It is good for a man to enjoy the fruit of his labor.

    - Ecclesiastes 5:18 // Then I realized that it is good and proper for a man to eat and drink, and to find satisfaction in his toilsome labor under the sun during the few days of life God has given him ... (NIV)

2. It is good for a man to enjoy his work.

    - Ecclesiastes 3:22 // So I saw that there is nothing better for a man than to enjoy his work, because that is his lot ... (NIV)

D. The Bible also has SERIOUS WARNINGS about money and possessions.

1. A warning about greed.

    - Luke 12:15 // Then he said to them, "Watch out! Be on your guard against all kinds of greed; a man's life does not consist in the abundance of his possessions." (NIV)

2. A warning about self-indulgence.

    - Amos 6:4-7 // How terrible for you who sprawl on ivory beds and lounge on your couches, eating the meat of tender lambs from the flock and of choice calves fattened in the stall ... You drink wine by the bowlful and perfume yourselves with fragrant lotions. You care nothing about the ruin of your nation. Therefore, you will be the first to be led away as captives. Suddenly, all your parties will end. (NLT)

3. A warning about the deceitfulness of riches.

    - Mark 4:19 // ... but the worries of the world, and the deceitfulness of riches, and the desires for other things enter in and choke the word, and it becomes unfruitful. (NASB)

4. A warning that God does not give dollars for spiritual cooperation.

    - 1 Timothy 6:5 // ... men of corrupt mind, who have been robbed of the truth and who think that godliness is a means to financial gain. (NIV)

5. A warning that money and possessions can become a substitute for God.

    - Mark 10:21-23 // Jesus looked at him and loved him. "One thing you lack," he said. "Go, sell everything you have and give to the poor, and you will have treasure in heaven. Then come, follow me."

      At this the man's face fell. He went away sad, because he had great wealth. Jesus looked around and said to his disciples, "How hard it is for the rich to enter the kingdom of God!" (NIV)

## II. 3 WORDS TO KEEP MONEY AND POSSESSIONS IN PROPER PERSPECTIVE

A. FREEDOM

- Hebrews 13:5 // Keep your lives free from the love of money and be content with what you have ... (NIV)

B. CONTENTMENT

- 1 Timothy 6:6 // But godliness with contentment is great gain. (NIV)

C. GENEROSITY

- 2 Corinthians 8:7 // But since you excel in everything—in faith, in speech, in knowledge, in complete earnestness and in the love we have kindled in you—see that you also excel in this grace of giving.

**COMPASSION EQUALS SPIRIT-PROMPTED GENEROSITY IN THE FACE OF GREED.**
Mark Batterson, *Primal*

**GAIN ALL YOU CAN, SAVE ALL YOU CAN, GIVE ALL YOU CAN.**
John Wesley

## TALK ABOUT IT

1. Think back over your life growing up as a boy and as a young man. What were some of the material possessions you thought you had to have to be happy and/or successful?

2. Have you ever purchased something that you believed would bring contentment but instead it brought stress into your life and stole your freedom?

3. Have you ever thought about giving generously to others but did not follow through? What held you back?

4. What are some things you could do now to create more financial margin in your life?

# NOTES

# NOTES

# DISCIPLINE

## I. WELCOME TO THE SECOND HALF

**HOW MUCH CAN YOU KNOW ABOUT YOURSELF IF YOU'VE NEVER BEEN IN A FIGHT?**
– Tyler Durdan from *Fight Club*, the movie

Consider it a sheer gift, friends, when tests and challenges come at you from all sides. You know that under pressure, your faith-life is forced into the open and shows its true colors. So don't try to get out of anything prematurely. Let it do its work so you become mature and well developed, not deficient in any way.
James 1:2-4, The Message

A. Pressure and challenges are good for us.

B. They are training grounds to develop us and proving grounds to reveal what is in us.

## II. RECAP OF THE FIRST SIX ROUNDS

A. ROUND ONE: 5 Rules & 5 Promises

B. ROUND TWO: Why Men Need to Fight

C. ROUND THREE: Our Common Enemy

D. ROUND FOUR: Character

E. ROUND FIVE: Margin

F. ROUND SIX: Money & Possessions

## III. THE PATH OF DISCIPLINE

> Just as there are physical paths that lead to predictable physical locations, there are other kinds of paths that are equally predictable.
>
> – Andy Stanley, *The Principle of the Path*

A. Discipline can come from two directions:

1. External Discipline: Control gained by enforcing obedience or order.

2. Internal Discipline (Self-Discipline): Restraint exercised over one's own impulses, emotions, or desires.

B. If external discipline is not matched with internal discipline, there will always be conflict.

C. A biblical view of discipline:

1. Discipline from God is evidence of a true believer.

   - Hebrews 12:5-8 // ... Endure hardship as discipline; God is treating you as sons. For what son is not disciplined by his father? If you are not disciplined (and everyone undergoes discipline), then you are illegitimate children and not true sons. (NIV)

2. God's discipline is good for us.

   - Hebrews 12:10 // God disciplines us for our good, that we may share in his holiness. (NIV)

   - Job 5:17 // Blessed is the man whom God corrects. So do not despise the discipline of the Almighty. (NIV)

3. Discipline is a paradox: It is painful and productive.

   - Hebrews 12:11 // No discipline seems pleasant at the time, but painful. Later on, however, it produces a harvest of righteousness and peace for those who have been trained by it. (NIV)

4. Lack of discipline could eliminate us from achieving authentic manhood.

   - 1 Corinthians 9:27 // ... I discipline my body and bring it under strict control, so that after preaching to others, I myself will not be disqualified. (NLT)

5. Discipline will involve self-denial and sacrifice.

   - Luke 9:23 // If anyone would come after me, he must deny himself and take up his cross daily and follow me. (NIV)

## IV. 10 KICK-STARTERS FOR A DISCIPLINED LIFE

(Adapted from *The Pillars of Christian Character* by John MacArthur.)

A. Start small.

1. Keep your environment clean: your desk, your room, your car.

2. Put things back in place when not in use.

3. Eliminate small distractions that grow into huge mountains.

B. Get organized.

1. Make a schedule.

2. Use a daily planning book or a time management program.

3. Build margin into your schedule or relationships will suffer.

4. At least use a simple To-Do List on a piece of scrap paper.

C. Don't constantly seek to be entertained.

1. Men are created to be producers, not just consumers.

2. When you have free time, seek to do things that are productive.

3. Read a good book; have a meaningful conversation; take a walk.

4. Do things that are challenging, stimulating and creative.

D. Be on time.

1. The proper use of time is a sign of spiritual wisdom.

- Ephesians 5:15-16 // Be careful how you walk, not as unwise men, but as wise, making the most of your time, because the days are evil. (NASB)

2. It shows that your desires and responsibilities are under control.

3. It acknowledges the importance of other people and the value of their time.

E. Keep your word.

1. Evaluate whether you have the time and ability to do something.

2. If you say you are going to do something, do it when and how you said you would do it.

F. Tackle the most difficult tasks first.

1. Focus your time and energy on the harder, high-priority tasks.

2. Many of the smaller, low-priority areas will fall into place.

G. If you start something, finish it.

1. Complete your own unfinished projects.

2. Enlist help if you're in over your head.

H. Accept correction.

1. Correction (external discipline) helps you develop self-discipline.

2. The Scriptures tell us that accepting discipline will also make us wise and that we will gain understanding.

- Proverbs 19:20 // Listen to counsel and accept discipline, that you may be wise the rest of your days. (NASB)

- Proverbs 15:32 // He who neglects discipline despises himself, but he who listens to reproof acquires understanding. (NASB)

I. Practice self-denial.

1. Learn to say no to your feelings and impulses.

2. Self-discipline will remind your body who is in charge.

J. Welcome responsibility.

   1. Evaluate opportunities and step into new challenges.

   2. This will force you to organize your life so you can deliver on what you committed to do.

## GUIDELINES FOR DISCUSSION

[1] DON'T RETEACH THE LESSON

[2] DON'T DOMINATE THE DISCUSSION

[3] BE SURE EVERYONE HAS A CHANCE TO TALK IF THEY WANT TO

## TALK ABOUT IT

1. Take a few minutes for introductions, especially if there are new men in your group.

2. Describe an experience you had with external discipline where obedience or order was enforced.

3. Talk about the paradox of discipline: How has discipline been painful and productive for you? How has self-denial and sacrifice paid off?

4. In what areas of your life would you say you are the most disciplined? The least disciplined?

5. Of the Ten Kick-Starters for a Disciplined Life, which one(s) will be the most difficult for you

# SPIRITUAL DISCIPLINE CHALLENGES

## STRENGTHEN YOUR CORE

Don't copy the behavior and customs of this world, but let God transform you into a new person by changing the way you think ...
Romans 12:2, NLT

Your word is a lamp to my feet and a light for my path.
Psalm 119:105, NIV

I rise before dawn and cry for help; I have put my hope in your word.
Psalm 119:147, NIV

It is God who arms me with strength and keeps my way secure.
Psalm 18:32, NIV

## CHALLENGE #1: READ THE SCRIPTURES

Train yourself to regularly read the Scriptures. The more you read , the more you see the bigger picture of life from God's perspective. Choose a strategy, set a goal and follow through:

☐ The OneYear Bible (oneyearbibleonline.com)

☐ Freestyle

- Read the story of Jesus in Matthew, Mark, Luke or John. (Suggestion: Start with John)
- Read a Proverb a day for 31 days.
- Read the shorter letters of Paul, James, Peter or John. (Colossians, Ephesians, Philippians, James, 1 Peter or 1 John, etc.)

## CHALLENGE #2: TIME ALONE WITH GOD

Luke 5:16 // Jesus often withdrew to lonely places and prayed. (NIV)

Mark 1:35 // Very early in the morning, while it was still dark, Jesus got up, left the house and went off to a solitary place, where he prayed. (NIV)

This was an important discipline to Jesus. You can follow His example by implementing one of these strategies:

- ☐ Freestyle
    - Good: Start your day by just praying through your To-Do List, seeking God's help and direction. End your day with a prayer of reflection and thanksgiving.
    - Better: Read a section of scripture, then pray about what you read and ask God to help you apply it to your day.
- ☐ Read, Pray & Journal
    - Pick a book of the Bible. (Suggestion: Start with something short like Colossians, Ephesians, Philippians, James, 1 Peter, or 1 John.)
    - On Day One, record the date and scripture passage in your journal or notebook.. For the passage, just choose a section that seems like a complete thought.
    - Read and write down your thoughts and applications.
    - List things you want to pray about.
    - Day Two and beyond, pick up where you left off the day before and repeat the process. Make notes of answers to prayer as you progress in this discipline.

## CHALLENGE #3: MEDITATE ON SCRIPTURE

Joshua 1:8 // Do not let this Book of the Law depart from your mouth; meditate on it day and night, so that you may be careful to do everything written in it. Then you will be prosperous and successful. (NIV)

- ☐ Pick a verse that is meaningful to you.
- ☐ Memorize it.
- ☐ Meditate on it. Make it personal and build it into your life.

# NOTES

# BROTHERHOOD

## I. ROUND 7 RECAP & SPIRITUAL DISCIPLINE CHALLENGES

A. Ten Kick-Starters for a Disciplined Life

*Affirmation without discipline is the beginning of delusion.* – Jim Rohn

B. Spiritual Discipline Challenges: Page 52

1. Read the Scriptures
2. Time Alone With God
3. Meditate on Scripture

C. Your Fight Plan: Page 95

- Write down your strategies and resources.
- *The discipline of writing something down is the first step toward making it happen.* – Lee Iacocca, Business Legend

## II. TRUE BROTHERHOOD

*In a perfect friendship – when the whole group is together, each bringing out all that is best, wisest, or funniest in all the others ... all are freemen and equals as if we had first met an hour ago, while at the same time an affection mellowed by the years enfolds us. Life – natural life – has no better gift to give.*

C.S. Lewis, *The Four Loves*

A. True brotherhood sharpens you.

- Proverbs 27:17 // As iron sharpens iron, so one man sharpens another. (NIV)

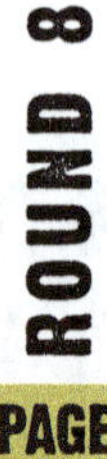

B. True brotherhood means connecting on a soul level.

- 1 Samuel 18:1 // ... the soul of Jonathan was knit to the soul of David, and Jonathan loved him as himself. (NASB)

1. Connecting on a soul level requires honesty and trust.

2. Honesty and trust require vulnerability.

3. Soul-level connections need time and practice.

C. Four Principles of Masculine Friendship

(From ***Tender Warrior*** by Stu Weber: The Four Piton Principles of Friendship)

1. Shared Values

    - 2 Corinthians 6:14 // Do not be yoked together with unbelievers. For what do righteousness and wickedness have in common? Or what fellowship can light have with darkness? (NIV)

2. Unselfish Love

    - 1 Samuel 18:3-4 // And Jonathan made a covenant with David because he loved him as himself. Jonathan took off the robe he was wearing and gave it to David, along with his tunic, and even his sword, his bow and his belt. (NIV)

3. Deep Loyalty

    - *A man-to-man friendship says, "I'll never walk out on you. Barring unrepentant sin against the Lord God, you'll never be able to do anything that will repulse me or break our fellowship."* – Stu Weber, *Tender Warrior*

4. Real Transparency

    - 1 Samuel 20:41 // David got up from the south side [of the stone] and bowed down before Jonathan three times, with his face to the ground. Then they kissed each other and wept together — but David wept the most. (NIV)

D. Five Degrees of Transparency
(From ***Why Am I Afraid to Tell You Who I Am?*** by John Powell)

1. The Cliché Level
2. The Fact Level
3. The Opinion Level
4. The Emotional Level
5. The Transparent Level

E. Common Ground

1. To one degree or another, we all struggle with the same things.

    - 1 Corinthians 10:13 // No temptation has seized you except what is common to man. And God is faithful; he will not let you be tempted beyond what you can bear. But when you are tempted, he will also provide a way out so that you can stand up under it. (NIV)

    - *Everything that's killing you is somewhere in the chest of every man you know.*
      – Stu Weber, *Tender Warrior*

2. The way out that God has provided is along the path of true brotherhood.

## III. FINAL THOUGHTS

2 Samuel 1:25-26 // How the mighty have fallen in battle! Jonathan lies slain on your heights. I grieve for you, Jonathan my brother; you were very dear to me. Your love for me was wonderful, more wonderful than that of women. (NIV)

A. For the man who is married, his wife is his most intimate friend.

B. A man has a need for companionship that cannot be met by a woman.

## TALK ABOUT IT

1. What is on your list of the top buddy movies of all time? What are some of the most memorable scenes?

2. How deep are your connections with other men?

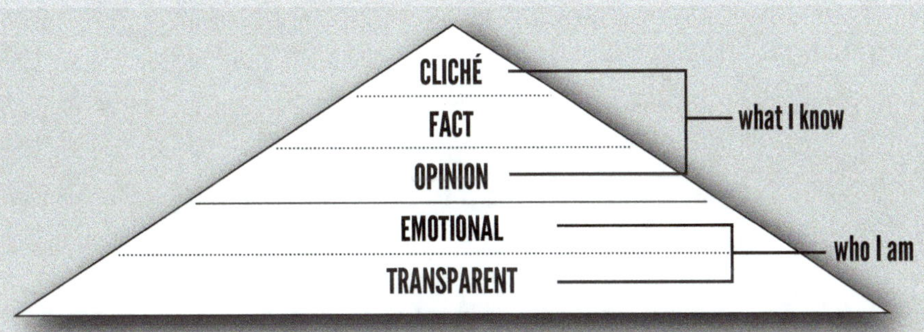


3. The good times. The tough times. The terrible times. Who has been there for you when you needed encouragement or correction? Describe the circumstances.

4. What do you think is standing in your way for more soul level connections with other men? How can you change that?

# NOTES

# PURITY

## I. ROUND 8 RECAP: TRUE BROTHERHOOD

A. True brotherhood sharpens you.

B. True brotherhood means connecting on a soul level.

- Requires honesty, trust and vulnerability along with time and practice.

C. Four Principles of Masculine Friendship:

1. Shared Values
2. Unselfish Love
3. Deep Loyalty
4. Real Transparency

D. We stand on common ground.

- To one degree or another, we all struggle with the same things.

E. A man has a need for companionship that cannot be met by a woman.

F. 3 Brotherhood Killers:

1. Individualism
2. Isolation
3. Privatization

## II. THE SPIRITUAL BATTLE FOR PURITY

A. Reminders from Round 3: Our Common Enemy

1. We are all engaged in a spiritual battle that affects every area of our life.

    - Ephesians 6:12 // For our struggle is not against flesh and blood, but against the rulers, against the authorities, against the powers of this dark world and against the spiritual forces of evil in the heavenly realms. (NIV)

2. Our common enemy is the Devil.

    - 1 Peter 5:8-9 // Be self-controlled and alert. Your enemy the devil prowls around like a roaring lion looking for someone to devour. Resist him, standing firm in the faith, because you know that your brothers throughout the world are undergoing the same kind of sufferings. (NIV)

B. We are not all fighting from the same position.

1. Some are "in Christ."

    - Romans 8:1 // Therefore, there is now no condemnation for those who are in Christ Jesus. (NIV)

2. Some are "cut-off" from Christ and separated from God.

    - Ephesians 4:18 // They are darkened in their understanding and separated from the life of God because of the ignorance that is in them due to the hardening of their hearts. (NIV)

C. The attack on purity has eternal implications.

1. For the man who is in Christ:

    - Can't lose his salvation
    - Can lose his peace and joy
    - Constantly doubting his salvation

- Can lose eternal rewards
- Can lose his influence, ministry, job, family
- Gives others reason to believe the claims of Christ are false
- Emotional, physical, relational and spiritual damage

2. For the man who is cut-off from Christ:
   - Heart will continue to harden toward God
   - The probability of ever turning to God will decrease
   - Emotional, physical, relational and spiritual damage
   - The eternal destiny of his soul is still at stake

D. More from Round Three: The Enemy's Strategy

1 John 2:15-17 // Do not love the world or anything in the world. If anyone loves the world, the love of the Father is not in him. For everything in the world – the cravings of sinful man, the lust of his eyes and the boasting of what he has and does – comes not from the Father but from the world. The world and its desires pass away, but the man who does the will of God lives forever. (NIV)

1. The Lust of the Flesh.
2. The Lust of the Eyes.
3. The Pride of Life.

## III. SATAN HAS OUR WORST INTEREST IN MIND

John 10:10 // The thief comes only to steal and kill and destroy; I have come that they may have life, and have it to the full. (NIV)

A. A 3-pronged attack on purity:

1. The Lust of the Flesh
    - Primarily a blow to the body
    - The objective is to pervert our physical desires
    - To pervert something is to use it in a way that distorts its created purpose
2. The Lust of the Eyes
    - Primarily a blow to the mind
    - It skews our perspective and clouds our vision
    - It is not only about what we see, but also about how we see
3. The Pride of Life
    - Deceives us into believing that our immoral behavior is not immoral
    - Keeps us from asking others for help
    - For the man who is cut-off from Christ it can be an eternal blow to his soul.
    - Romans 1:20-32

D. What the enemy can and cannot do:

1. He cannot make us do anything.
2. He can corrupt our thoughts to manipulate our feelings which can affect our behavior.

## IV. THE PATH OF PURITY

1 Timothy 4:12 // Don't let anyone look down on you because you are young, but set an example for the believers in speech, in life, in love, in faith and in purity. (NIV)

A. Guard your mind.

- Romans 12:2 // Do not conform any longer to the pattern of this world, but be transformed by the renewing of your mind ... (NIV)
- 2 Corinthians 10:5 // We take captive every thought to make it obedient to Christ. (NIV)
- Colossians 3:2 // Set your minds on things above, not on earthly things. (NIV)

B. Train your eyes.

- Psalm 101:3 // I will refuse to look at anything vile and vulgar ... (NLT)
- Proverbs 23:26 // My son, give me your heart and let your eyes keep to my ways. (NIV)

C. Honor God with your body.

1 Corinthians 6:18-20 // Flee from sexual immorality. All other sins a man commits are outside his body, but he who sins sexually sins against his own body. Do you not know that your body is a temple of the Holy Spirit, who is in you, whom you have received from God? You are not your own; you were bought at a price. Therefore honor God with your body. (NIV)

1. Our body is the temple of the Holy Spirit.
2. What we choose to do with our body can either restrict or release the power of the Holy Spirit.
3. Where do you draw the line?
    - Ephesians 5:3 // But among you there must not be even a hint of sexual immorality, or of any kind of impurity, or of greed, because these are improper for God's holy people. (NIV)

D. Meditate on scripture.

- Psalm 119:11 // I have hidden your word in my heart that I might not sin against you. (NIV)
- Philippians 4:8 // Finally, brothers, whatever is true, whatever is noble, whatever is right, whatever is pure, whatever is lovely, whatever is admirable – if anything is excellent or praiseworthy – think about such things. (NIV)

E. Avoid isolation.

- Ecclesiastes 4:9-10 // Two are better than one, because they have a good return for their work: If one falls down, his friend can help him up. But pity the man who falls and has no one to help him up! (NIV)

F. Feed your mind with books and knowledge supported by the timeless truth of the Scriptures.

1. General books on a healthy perspective of sex:

   *The Sexual Man* by Dr. Archibald Hunt

   *The Act of Marriage: The Beauty of Sexual Love* by Tim & Beverly LaHaye

2. Specific books on sexual impurity and sexual addiction:

   *Every Man's Battle* by Stephen Arterburn & Fred Stoeker

   *Healing the Wounds of Sexual Addiction* by Dr. Mark Laaser

   *Don't Call It Love: Recovery from Sexual Addiction* by Dr. Patrick Carnes

   *Out of the Shadows: Understanding Sexual Addiction* by Dr. Patrick Carnes

G. Seek professional help.

- Lay Counseling (Trained by Professionals)
- Professional Christian-Based Counseling
- Recovery Groups like Celebrate Recovery

## SEXUAL ADDICTION VS. NORMAL SEXUALITY

From *Healing the Wounds of Sexual Addiction*, by Dr. Mark Laaser

| BEHAVIORS & THOUGHTS | SEX ADDICTS | NON-SEX ADDICTS |
|---|---|---|
| Thinks about sex | Constantly | Occasionally |
| Encounters sexual stimuli, such as pornography or an attractive person | Initiates a cycle of sexual thoughts and hoped-for sexual activities. Disregards all moral and spiritual boundaries. | Notes the stimulus and moves on to other thoughts. Considers all moral and spiritual boundaries. |
| Masturbation | Becomes a habitual pattern used to medicate feelings. | Experiments but doesn't allow it to become a pattern. |
| Experience of sexual sin | Goes through a cycle of guilt and shame and repeats sin. | Repents, confesses, and learns from the experience. |
| Marital sexuality | Selfish use of spouse to meet needs, including the need to avoid feelings. | Selfless expression of the deepest levels of emotional and spiritual intimacy. |

## TALK ABOUT IT

1. What has had a positive influence in your fight for purity? What has had a negative influence?
2. Other than sex, or in addition to sex, what issues have you had to face in the fight for purity?
3. What would you say to someone who has wandered off the path of purity and feels trapped?
4. Of the seven things listed to stay on a path of purity, which one(s) do you need to implement this week?

# NOTES

# NOTES

# MARRIAGE

## I. ROUND 9 RECAP: PURITY

A. The battle for purity is a spiritual battle with eternal implications.

B. Seven things to stay on a path of purity:

1. Guard your mind
2. Train your eyes
3. Avoid isolation
4. Honor God with your body
5. Meditate on Scripture
6. Feed your mind with truth
7. Seek professional help

C. We are called to be different — to be blameless and pure.

- Philippians 2:14-15 // Do everything without complaining or arguing, so that you may become blameless and pure, children of God without fault in a crooked and depraved generation, in which you shine like stars in the universe ... (NIV)

D. The principle of sowing and reaping.

- Galatians 6:7-8 // Do not be deceived: God cannot be mocked. A man reaps what he sows. The one who sows to please his sinful nature, from that nature will reap destruction; the one who sows to please the Spirit, from the Spirit will reap eternal life. (NIV)

## II. FOUNDATIONAL PRINCIPLES OF MARRIAGE

A. The marriage relationship was the first institution created by God.

- Genesis 1:26-27 // Then God said, "Let us make man in our image, in our likeness, and let them rule over the fish of the sea and the birds of the air, over the livestock, over all the earth, and over all the creatures that move along the ground." So God created man in his own image, in the image of God he created him; male and female he created them. (NIV)

B. The marriage relationship is not a competition.

- Genesis 2:23-24 // The man said, "This is now bone of my bones and flesh of my flesh; she shall be called woman, for she was taken out of man." For this reason a man will leave his father and mother and be united to his wife, and they will become one flesh. (NIV)

**TWO BECOMING ONE FLESH IMPLICATIONS**

**WHEN THERE IS CONFLICT IN YOUR MARRIAGE, IF YOUR GOAL IS TO WIN, YOU WILL ALWAYS LOSE.**

C. Men and women are equal, but husbands and wives have different roles.

1. The role of the husband is HEAD.

   - Ephesians 5:23 // The husband is the head of the wife as Christ is the head of the church ... (NIV)

   - Ephesians 5:25 // Husbands, love your wives, just as Christ loved the church and gave himself up for her ... (NIV)

     - This is a description of a servant-leader.

   - As the head, the husband is responsible for the overall health of the marriage.

     - Genesis 3:9-12 // But the Lord God called to the man, "Where are you? ... Have you eaten from the tree that I commanded you not to eat from?"

       The man said, "The woman you put here with me – she gave me some fruit from the tree, and I ate it." (NIV)

   - As men, we will have to fight to accept responsibility and lead courageously in our marriage, but the fight is not against our wives. The fight is against ourselves and against our common enemy, the Devil.

2. The role of the wife is HELPER.

    - Genesis 2:18 // The Lord God said, "It is not good for the man to be alone. I will make a helper suitable for him." (NIV)

    - This role does not devalue the woman. The word that is translated "helper" is used to describe God the Father, God the Son, God the Holy Spirit, and the woman.

    - Ephesians 5:24 // Now as the church submits to Christ, so also wives should submit to their husbands in everything. (NIV)

> Wives, understand and support your husbands in ways that show your support for Christ. The husband provides leadership to his wife the way Christ does to his church, not by domineering but by cherishing. So just as the church submits to Christ as he exercises such leadership, wives should likewise submit to their husbands.
>
> Ephesians 5:22-24, The Message

C. Marriage is a covenant relationship.

1. Biblically it is defined as a solemn and binding relationship meant to last a lifetime.

2. From the Hebrew word "berith" which means "to cut."

## III. WHAT ABOUT DIVORCE?

A. What Jesus said about it:

1. Matthew 19:4-6 // [Jesus said,] " ... Therefore what God has joined together, let man not separate." (NIV)

2. Matthew 19:7-8 // "Why then," they asked, "did Moses command that a man give his wife a certificate of divorce and send her away?"

   Jesus replied, "Moses permitted you to divorce your wives because your hearts were hard. But it was not this way from the beginning." (NIV)

> Moses provided for divorce as a concession to your hard heartedness, but it is not part of God's original plan. I'm holding you to the original plan ...
>
> Matthew 19:8, The Message

3. Matthew 19:9 // Whoever divorces his wife, except for sexual immorality, and marries another, commits adultery. (HCSB)

B. Divorce was not part of God's original plan.

1. The only concession Jesus made for divorce is sexual immorality, or adultery.

2. God's original design for marriage: Do it right and do it once.

C. Five key moves in the face of divorce:

1. Accept responsibility.

2. Seek wise counsel.

3. Seek forgiveness from God and others.

   - 1 John 1:9 // If we confess our sins, he is faithful and just and will forgive us our sins and purify us from all unrighteousness. (NIV)

   - Romans 8:1 // There is now no condemnation for those who are in Christ Jesus. (NIV)

   - James 4:6 // God opposes the proud but gives grace to the humble. (NIV)

4. Seek soul-level connections with other men.

    - Ecclesiastes 4:9-10 // Two are better than one ... If one falls down, his friend can help him up. But pity the man who falls and has no one to help him up! (NIV)

5. Seek to honor the sanctity of marriage.

## TALK ABOUT IT

1. Talk about your marriage role models. How have they helped or hurt you?

2. How have you seen the roles of a husband being the head and the wife being a helper modeled in a negative way? Talk about real or fictional examples.

3. Ephesians 5:21 says, "Submit to one another out of reverence for Christ." How can this principle of mutual submission help us fulfill our role as head and more closely follow the example of Jesus who loved the church and gave himself up for it?

4. What benefits or challenges do you see in implementing the five key moves in the face of divorce?

# NOTES

# NOTES

# LEGACY

## I. ACCEPT RESPONSIBILITY

A. God will hold us accountable.

- Malachi 2:13-14 // You cover the altar of the Lord with tears, with weeping and with groaning, because He no longer regards the offering or accepts it with favor from your hand. Yet you say, "For what reason?" Because the Lord has been a witness between you and the wife of your youth, against whom you have dealt treacherously, though she is your companion and your wife by covenant. (NASB)

B. My Covenant Promise:

I promise to be your servant-leader; to love you as Christ loved the church and gave himself up for it. I promise to lead you, to protect you and to provide for you. I promise to honor you through my thoughts, through my words, and through my deeds. I promise to never leave you. You are God's precious gift to me, and I pledge my faithfulness to you until we are parted by death.

THIS IS MY SOLEMN VOW.

## II. MARITAL CONFLICT IS CREATED IN ONE OF TWO WAYS:

A. Failure to care.

- Couples fail to make each other happy.
- They are frustrated because their needs are not being met.

B. Failure to protect.

- Couples make each other unhappy.
- They are deliberately hurting each other.

## III. THE NEEDS OF HUSBANDS AND WIVES

A. Husbands and wives are typically willing to do for each other what they appreciate the most.

B. A big lesson to learn: My needs are not her needs.

C. One of the prime objectives of a husband is to live with his wife in an understanding way.

- 1 Peter 3:7 // You husbands ... live with your wives in an understanding way, as with a weaker vessel, since she is a woman; and grant her honor as a fellow heir of the grace of life, so that your prayers may not be hindered. (NASB)

D. On average, the top five needs of men are:[1]

1. Sexual Fulfillment
2. Recreational Companionship
3. An Attractive Spouse
4. Domestic Support
5. Admiration or Respect

F. On average, the top five needs of women are:[2]

1. Affection
2. Conversation
3. Honesty and Openness
4. Financial Support
5. Family Commitment

---

[1] Willard Harley, *"His Needs, Her Needs."*

[2] Willard Harley

G. The Five Love Languages:[3]

1. Words of Affirmation
2. Quality Time
3. Receiving Gifts
4. Acts of Service
5. Physical Touch

## IV. THE LEGACY WE LEAVE

A. A primary purpose in the marriage relationship is to release a healthy next generation.

- Genesis 1:28 // And God blessed them; and God said to them, "Be fruitful and multiply, and fill the earth, and subdue it ... " (NASB)

B. The health of a generation depends on an authentic relationship with God.

- Deuteronomy 6:1-2 // ... so that you, your children and their children after them may fear the Lord your God as long as you live by keeping all his decrees and commands that I give you, and so that you may enjoy long life. (NIV)

C. An authentic relationship with God for your children begins with you.

- Deuteronomy 6:5-6 // Love the Lord your God with all your heart and with all your soul and with all your strength. These commandments that I give you today are to be upon your hearts. (NIV)

[3] Gary Chapman, *"The 5 Love Languages."*

D. You must be intentional.

- Deuteronomy 6:7-8 // Impress them on your children. Talk about them when you sit at home and when you walk along the road, when you lie down and when you get up. Tie them as symbols on your hands and bind them on your foreheads. Write them on the doorframes of your houses and on your gates. (NIV)

1. If those daily times—both quality and quantity—do not exist, then you must create them.

2. Be strategic.

3. How will you impress God's truth on your children?

4. Use symbolism and ceremony to mark events and clarify promises.

5. Share your successes.

6. Share your failures and ask forgiveness.

E. Robertson McQuilken: *A Promise Kept*

SPIRITUAL and RELATIONAL GROWTH CHART

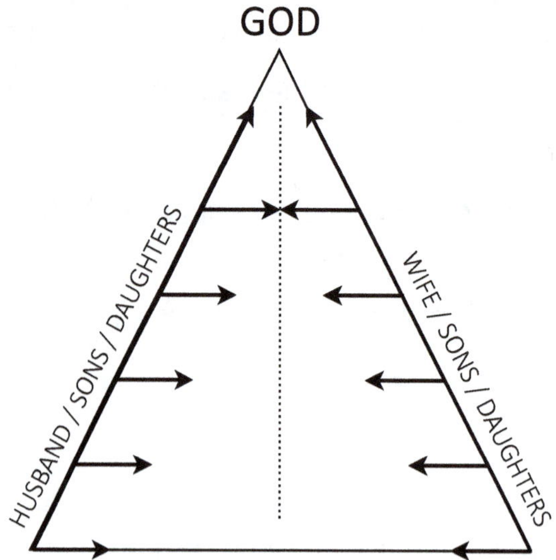


## TALK ABOUT IT

1. Take a look at the needs we listed for men and women from Dr. Willard Harley's research. Are the five for men true for you? If not, what would your list in order of importance look like?

2. How do the needs listed for women stack up with your wife? What do you think her top five are in order of importance?

3. What do you think your primary love language is? What about your wife?

4. As husbands and wives grow closer to God they typically grow closer to each other. The same is true for and with their children. Where do think you and your family are on the Spiritual and Relational Growth Chart in the diagram above?

5. If you have never been married, how can you benefit from what we learned about marriage and the legacy we can leave?

# NOTES

# NOTES

# FAITH

## I. INTRODUCTION: A FATHER-DAUGHTER DATE

## II. THE GOOD FIGHT OF FAITH

A. A strong faith is an active faith.

B. If you reject this principle, you WILL wipeout.

- 1 Timothy 1:18-19 // Timothy, my son, I give you this instruction in keeping with the prophecies once made about you, so that by following them you may fight the good fight, holding on to faith and a good conscience. Some have rejected these and so have shipwrecked their faith. (NIV)

C. Jesus hates faith that is stale and stagnant.

- Revelation 3:15-16 // I know your deeds, that you are neither cold nor hot. I wish you were either one or the other! So, because you are lukewarm—neither hot nor cold—I am about to spit you out of my mouth. (NIV)

D. Strong faith means doing what Jesus said.

- John 14:15 // If you love me, you will obey what I command. (NIV)
- Luke 6:49 // The one who hears my words and does not put them into practice is like a man who built a house on the ground without a foundation. The moment the torrent struck that house, it collapsed and its destruction was complete. (NIV)

## III. THE FOUNDATION OF OUR FAITH

> For no one can lay any foundation other than the one already laid, which is Jesus Christ.
>
> 1 Corinthians 3:11, NIV

A. Compared to God' s standard of righteousness we all miss the mark.

- Romans 3:23 // There is no difference, for all have sinned and fall short of the glory of God. (NIV)
- Romans 6:23 // For the wages of sin is death ... (NIV)

B. The only acceptable sacrifice for our sin is the blood of Jesus.

- Hebrews 9:22 // The law requires that nearly everything be cleansed with blood, and without the shedding of blood there is no forgiveness. (NIV)
- Romans 5:8 // But God demonstrates his own love for us in this: While we were still sinners, Christ died for us. (NIV)

C. The one and only path of forgiveness and salvation is Jesus Christ.

- Acts 4:12 // Salvation is found in no one else, for there is no other name under heaven given to men by which we must be saved. (NIV)

## IV. CULTURE CLASH

> We preach Christ crucified: a stumbling block to Jews and foolishness to Gentiles.
> 1 Corinthians 1:23, NIV

A. The message of Christ may clash with some in your own family.

- Matthew 10:34-36 // Do not suppose that I have come to bring peace to the earth. I did not come to bring peace, but a sword ... a man's enemies will be the members of his own household. (NIV)

B. If you identify yourself with Christ there is a chance that some will hate you.

- John 15:18-19 // If the world hates you, keep in mind that it hated me first. If you belonged to the world, it would love you as its own. As it is, you do not belong to the world, but I have chosen you out of the world. That is why the world hates you. (NIV)

C. If you want to be like Christ, to be godly, you can expect to be persecuted.

- 2 Timothy 3:12 // Everyone who wants to live a godly life in Christ Jesus will be persecuted. (NIV)

**WARNING!**

Persecution can be a reaction to our arrogance and self-righteousness.

But how is it to your credit if you receive a beating for doing wrong and endure it? But if you suffer for doing good and you endure it, this is commendable before God.

1 Peter 2:20, NIV

## V. FINAL THOUGHTS

A. Remember that you are ultimately fighting against our common enemy the Devil.

1. Review the 8 Moves to Gain Position Over Our Common Enemy in Round 3.

    - 1 Peter 5:8 // Your enemy the devil prowls around like a roaring lion looking for someone to devour. (NIV)

2. Tap into the power of prayer.

    - James 4:7 // Submit yourselves, then, to God. Resist the devil, and he will flee from you. (NIV)

B. Remember what is ultimately at stake: The souls of mankind

- 1 Timothy 6:12 // Fight the good fight of the faith. Take hold of the eternal life to which you were called when you made your good confession in the presence of many witnesses. (NIV)

## ONE MAN'S FIGHT | ONE MAN'S LEGACY

Five times I received from the Jews the forty lashes minus one.
Three times I was beaten with rods, once I was stoned ...

2 Corinthians 11:24-25, NIV

I bear on my body the marks of Jesus.

Galatians 6:17, NIV

I have fought the good fight, I have finished the race, I have kept the faith.

2 Timothy 4:7, NIV

## TALK ABOUT IT

1. Where do you see yourself in fighting The Good Fight of Faith?

2. When did you put your faith in in Jesus? What is your story?

3. What have been some of your biggest obstacles in fighting The Good Fight of Faith?

4. Has your faith clashed with people in your family, your community or in your workplace?

5. Looking back over all 12 Rounds of this series, what has helped you the most? Why and how?

# HOW TO BEGIN THE GOOD FIGHT OF FAITH

## 5 Questions to Determine if You Are a Contender:

1. Do you believe that no matter how good, moral or religious you are that you still miss the mark and you will never measure up to God's standard of righteousness in and of yourself?
2. Do you believe that Jesus Christ is God's one and only Son and that there is no other way to have a relationship with God apart from Him?
3. Do you believe that the sacrifice of Jesus was God's payment in full for your sin?
4. Do you believe that Jesus died, was buried and raised from the dead?

> Saying yes to all of the above questions does not make you a follower of Jesus. It only means you have your information correct and you have an appreciation for who Christ is. Your answer to Question 5 determines whether or not you are a contender in The Good Fight of Faith.

5. Has there ever been a time in your life when you repented of your sins, put your faith in Jesus Christ and submitted to His will? If not, then why not now?

## The Good Fight of Faith Starts With Prayer

There is no magic phrase to say or a specific set of sentences to pray. In your own words, just tell God that you know you have fallen short of His mark of righteousness—that you are a sinner. Thank Him for sacrificing His only Son Jesus for your sins. Ask Him to forgive you and tell Him you want follow Him in everything you do.

## Go the Distance

Posers and pretenders just do lip service. True contenders follow through with real service to God and others. Connect with others in authentic community. That means committing to a church and small group environments within that church. Go all in!

Go public with your faith. Get baptized now that your faith is real. If you did it before you submitted to God's will and before you put your faith in Christ, it was just a religious ritual. Do it now for the true meaning of a man who has put his faith in Jesus—a man who has died to his old life where he was cut-off from Christ and has risen to live a new life in Christ.

# NOTES

# NOTES

I do not run like someone running aimlessly. I do not fight like a boxer beating the air. No, I strike a blow to my body and make it my slave so that after I have preached to others, I myself will not be disqualified for the prize.

1 Corinthians 9:26-27

**YOUR FIGHT PLAN** will be a work in progress. As you fully engage in the sessions and participate in the discussions you will feel prompted to make some personal notes about your life and the actions you need to take to keep moving forward in your quest for authentic manhood.

IF YOUR FIGHT PLAN IS GOING TO BE EFFECTIVE, YOU MUST ...

- MAKE IT PERSONAL. It should be a tool that challenges YOU with a personal call to action. Customize it. Make it YOUR Fight Plan. It has to be a tool that fits you.
- BE SPECIFIC. Target specific strengths and weaknesses. Use words and phrases that focus your attention on things that matter the most in your life and areas where you struggle the most.
- BE INTENTIONAL. Set goals and deadlines. Decide now to accept responsibility for your actions regardless of what other people do.

ORGANIZE YOUR NOTES INTO THESE CATEGORIES:

1. THINGS I NEED TO FIGHT FOR. What really matters the most? List your primary relationships, core values, and goals (short and long-term).
2. MY OPPONENTS & MY WEAKNESSES. List unhealthy tendencies and areas where you struggle the most. What warning signs are you seeing?
3. STRATEGIES & RESOURCES. List things you can do that will put you on a healthy path today, this week, this month or this year. List things that need to become a habit in your life. List things that need to be eliminated. List books you need to read, classes you need to attend or help you need to seek.
4. CORNER MEN. Which men do you need in your corner to help you fight? Whose corner do you need to be in? Make a list. Initiate the conversation(s).
5. SUMMARY. Begin to list the actions you will take to address your weaknesses and strengthen your core. Your plan will probably be a series of rough drafts before it is complete.

FINAL DRAFT:

Synthesize your notes into a personal format. Update it regularly. Share it with trustworthy friends who will hold you accountable—your corner men.

THINGS I NEED TO FIGHT FOR

MY OPPONENTS & MY WEAKNESSES

STRATEGIES & RESOURCES

CORNER MEN

SUMMARY

| MOST IMPORTANT THINGS IN LIFE | VICES |
| --- | --- |
| | |
| | |
| | |
| | |
| | |
| | |
| | |
| | |
| | |
| | |
| | |
| | |
| | |
| | |
| | |

Are the vices you hold onto worth trading for the most important things in your life?
—Chad Robichaux

# MY FIGHT PLAN

# MY FIGHT PLAN

# RECOMMENDED READING

## Books referenced in the 12 Rounds of Fight Club:

*Locking Arms: God's Design for Masculine Friendships* – Stu Weber

*Tender Warrior* – Stu Weber

*Louder Than Words* – Andy Stanley

*The Principal of the Path* – Andy Stanley

*How Full Is Your Bucket?* – Tom Rath & Donald Clifton

*Little House on the Freeway: Help for the Hurried Home* – Tim Kimmel

*Primal: A Quest for the Lost Soul of Christianity* – Mark Batterson

*The Pillars of Christian Character* – John MacArthur

*The Four Loves* – C.S. Lewis

*Every Man's Battle* – Stephen Arterburn & Fred Stoeker

*His Needs, Her Needs* – Willard F. Harley

*The Five Love Languages* – Gary Chapman

*Raising a Modern Day Knight* – Robert Lewis

## Other related books:

*Carry a Big Stick: The Uncommon Heroism of Theodore Roosevelt* – George Grant

*Sacred Marriage* – Gary Thomas

*Sacred Parenting* – Gary Thomas

*Raising Kids for True Greatness* – Tim Kimmel

*Grace Based Parenting* – Tim Kimmel

*Boys Should Be Boys* – Meg Meeker

*Strong Fathers, Strong Daughters* – Meg Meeker

*The Sexual Man* – Dr. Archibald Hunt

*The Act of Marriage: The Beauty of Sexual Love* – Tim & Beverly LaHaye

*Healing the Wounds of Sexual Addiction* – Dr. Mark Laaser

*Don't Call It Love: Recovery from Sexual Addiction* – Dr. Patrick Carnes

*Out of the Shadows: Understanding Sexual Addiction* – Dr. Patrick Carnes

www.ingramcontent.com/pod-product-compliance
Lightning Source LLC
LaVergne TN
LVHW081633120826
845149LV00025B/1905

* 9 7 9 8 9 9 2 1 5 3 8 1 1 *